As of January 6, 2012, this guidance applies to federal savings associations in addition to national banks.*

Comptroller of the Currency
Administrator of National Banks

I0448190

Asset Management

Comptroller's Handbook

December 2000

AM
Asset Management

As of January 6, 2012, this guidance applies to federal savings associations in addition to national banks.*

Asset Management   Table of Contents

As of January 6, 2012, this guidance applies to federal savings associations in addition to national banks.*

Introduction

The Office of the Comptroller of the Currency (OCC) defines asset management as the business of providing financial products or services to a third party for a fee or commission. The supervision of asset management activities is an important component of the OCC's safety and soundness supervisory framework. This booklet provides an overview of the asset management business, its risks, and sound risk management processes. It also describes the OCC's supervisory philosophy and processes, and how they are applied to the asset management activities of national banks, including limited purpose trust banks.

The OCC is publishing a series of asset management booklets, of which this booklet is the lead. Examiners use asset management booklets when reviewing asset management products and services; national banks use the booklets to help them manage these products and services. The examination procedures herein are designed for use by OCC examiners in large banks and, as needed, in community banks. In community banks, the procedures supplement the "Community Bank Fiduciary Activities Supervision" booklet of the *Comptroller's Handbook*.

In addition to the asset management booklets, other booklets from the *Comptroller's Handbook* provide important supervisory guidance applicable to asset management activities. They are referred to throughout this booklet, and a list of them is provided on the "References" pages.

Industry Characteristics

For the past quarter century, the asset management business has been rapidly growing and evolving, helped by demographic, technological, regulatory, and global economic trends. The traditionally conservative fiduciary business of national banks is undergoing a transition to a dynamic and highly competitive asset management business.

Hallmarks of the evolution of the asset management industry include:

- Tremendous product demand from an increasingly sophisticated and globally oriented client;

- Intense competition from other financial service providers, such as investment companies, insurance companies, and brokerage firms;

- Expansion of bank powers through the removal of most of the Glass-Steagall Act restrictions and other financial modernization initiatives;

- Rapid globalization of financial instruments and markets;

- Significant industry consolidation through mergers and acquisitions; and

- The development of complex and rapidly changing product distribution and information technologies.

Asset management activities expose national banks to an increasingly broad range of risk factors and thus reinforce the importance of maintaining sound risk management processes. National banks must have the ability to effectively identify, measure, control, and monitor risks in their asset management businesses. Because most of these risks arise from off-balance-sheet activities, they are not easily identified and measured using traditional financial reporting systems.

Many national banks are marketing new and complex financial products and services to strengthen their competitiveness, meet growing customer demand, and generate additional sources of noninterest income. Declining interest margins and the desire for a stable and diversified revenue stream have caused banks to look for ways to increase the level and source of noninterest income. Asset management products and services are filling this need and have become, or are becoming, a significant contributor to total revenue and the overall profitability of many national banks.

National banks have made strategic acquisitions of, and alliances with, domestic and international financial services companies, such as brokerage, insurance, investment banking, and investment advisory firms. These transactions are driven by a need to expand or fill product lines; extend distribution channels and market penetration; improve cost efficiency; and acquire additional expertise, talent, and technology. At the same time, other banks have made strategic decisions to focus on traditional fiduciary lines of business.

Products and Services

Asset management activities include traditional fiduciary services, retail brokerage, investment company services, and custody and security-holder services. The distribution channels for asset management products and services vary according to the size, complexity, financial capacity, and geographic characteristics of each institution. They may be provided in a centralized division of the bank, through several divisions in different geographical locations, in bank operating subsidiaries and other affiliates, and through arrangements with unaffiliated third parties.

For example, a large banking company may establish an asset management group consisting of several interlocking divisions, branches, subsidiaries, and affiliates that provide a broad range of asset management products and services on a global scale. A small community bank may simply operate a separate "trust" division that provides traditional fiduciary services and may also provide access to retail brokerage services through an unaffiliated third-party vendor located within the bank's branch network.

Product demand and technological advancements are rapidly changing the structures of financial markets and the means of product distribution. The globalization and deregulation of financial markets have compelled many larger banks to offer products and services in a number of markets around the world. The Internet is but one example of a technology that is altering the product distribution landscape for all banks and creating challenging risks for the industry.

In response to the demand from and competition for the wealthy individual client, many national banks offer what has been traditionally referred to as "private banking services." In many respects, private banking is the same business today that it was in the past – the high-quality and confidential provision of finance-related services to wealthy individuals and their businesses. Today, private banking is one of the fastest growing segments of the financial services industry. The growth in demand for these services has been driven by the tremendous generation of wealth and significant technological advancements achieved over the past decade. Private banking services will be addressed in the "Personal Financial Services" booklet of the *Comptroller's Handbook*, which has yet to be published as of this booklet's publication date.

Fiduciary Services

Fiduciary services offered by national banks have evolved into a comprehensive and integrated selection of financial products and services that permit banks to compete with other financial service providers, such as brokerage firms, investment companies, investment advisers, and insurance companies. Traditional fiduciary services include personal trust and estate administration, retirement plan services, investment management services, and corporate trust administration.

National banks also provide other fee- or transaction-based fiduciary-related services, such as financial planning; cash management; tax advisory and preparation; and advice on, and execution of, financial risk management products, such as derivatives. Fiduciary services are provided through internal bank divisions, subsidiaries (including separately chartered trust banks), other affiliates, and third-party service arrangements.

The increasing importance of fee income is a key factor in the evolution of fiduciary services. Rapid technological advances, state legislatures adopting reasonable compensation statutes, and a management focus on generating additional revenue sources have enabled banks to base the prices of their products and services on actual delivery costs and internal risk/return profitability standards. Competitive and innovative fiduciary products and services give banks the opportunity to increase and diversify revenue streams.

Custody and Security-holder Services

National banks have long provided custody and security-holder services incidental to the delivery of other fiduciary services. In recent years, the institutional side of the custody business has become concentrated in a few large banking companies through mergers and acquisitions. Related services include custody, safekeeping, payment, settlement, record keeping, transfer agent, securities lending, and other reporting functions for security instruments, such as equities, debt, and related hybrids. Banks may serve in a trustee or agent capacity with or without investment discretion authority. These services may be provided for the issuer or the holder of securities and include both domestic and international clients. Refer to the "Custody Services" and "Corporate Trust" booklets of the *Comptroller's Handbook* (neither booklet has been published as of this booklet's publication date) for more information about these activities.

Retail Securities Brokerage

Retail securities brokerage is an important and growing line of business for many banks, particularly large banking companies. Banks offer retail brokerage services to meet their clients' investment needs, maintain and strengthen customer relationships, and generate fee income. Retail brokerage services include the sale of equities, fixed-income products, mutual funds, annuities, cash management sweep accounts, and other types of investment instruments. Service capacities range from full-service brokerage that provides clients investment advice to discount brokerage that provides trade execution on an unsolicited basis. Large banking companies utilize their retail banking network as a marketing mechanism for both proprietary and nonproprietary investment products.

Investment Company Services

National banks have long provided financial services to investment companies, including registered and unregistered companies. The provision of investment company services is now a strategic line of business and income generator for many banks. Investment company services include fund administration, investment advisory, custody, and transfer agency activities. Financial subsidiaries of national banks are permitted to underwrite and distribute shares of registered investment companies.

Regulatory Framework

As the primary regulator of national banks, the OCC has the responsibility for evaluating the consolidated risk profile of a bank, including risks associated with asset management. National banks may, however, provide asset management products and services that are functionally regulated by another federal or state agency. Such agencies have the primary responsibility to supervise the functional activity (such as securities brokerage or investment advisory services) and interpret and enforce applicable laws and regulations under their jurisdiction.

The OCC is responsible for assessing the potential material risks posed to the bank by functionally regulated activities conducted by the bank or a functionally regulated entity, and for determining compliance with applicable legal requirements under the OCC's jurisdiction. A key part of this responsibility is evaluating a national bank's systems for managing risks that a functionally regulated activity poses to the bank. The OCC's policy on functional supervision will be included in the "Bank Supervision Process" booklet of the *Comptroller's Handbook*, which has yet to be published as of this booklet's publication date.

For a list of the primary laws and regulations applicable to asset management activities, see this booklet's "References" pages.

Fiduciary Powers

The statutory authority for national banks to exercise fiduciary powers is 12 USC. 92a, Trust Powers. Under section 92a(a) the OCC is authorized to permit national banks, when not in contravention of state or local law, to exercise eight expressly identified fiduciary powers and to act in any other fiduciary capacity in which state banks, trust companies, or other corporations that come into competition with national banks are permitted to act under the laws of the state in which the national bank is located. Under section 92a(b), whenever state law permits state institutions that compete with national banks to exercise any or all of the fiduciary powers listed in section 92a(a), a national bank's exercise of those powers is deemed not to be in contravention of state or local law under section 92a.

Section 92a does not expressly address the extent to which a national bank may conduct a multi-state fiduciary business. Many bank holding companies conduct multi-state fiduciary operations through separate bank or trust company subsidiaries chartered in different states. While the Riegle-Neal Interstate Banking and Branching Efficiency Act of 1994 facilitated the consolidation of multi-state fiduciary operations by permitting interstate bank mergers, it did not define the scope of a national bank's multi-state fiduciary authority.

The OCC has since issued three interpretive letters that address multi-state fiduciary operations. OCC Interpretive Letter 695, dated December 8, 1995, concluded that a national bank with its main office in one state may act in a fiduciary capacity in any other state that permits its own in-state fiduciaries to act in that capacity, including at non-branch trust offices. In Interpretive Letters 866 and 872, dated October 8, 1999, and October 28, 1999, respectively, the OCC further clarified that a national bank that acts in a fiduciary capacity in one state may market its fiduciary services to customers in other states, solicit business from them, and act as a fiduciary for customers located in other states. Please refer to the full text of these letters for additional information concerning multi-state fiduciary operations.

Fiduciary powers may be authorized for, and conducted in, a full-service commercial bank, a subsidiary, or a special purpose bank whose charter is limited to fiduciary activities. In order to exercise fiduciary powers, a national bank must submit an application to the OCC and obtain prior approval from the agency; in certain circumstances, it may be required merely to file a notice with the agency. The OCC generally approves fiduciary applications if the bank is operated in a satisfactory manner, the proposed activities comply with applicable law, and the bank retains qualified fiduciary management. OCC procedures governing the review and approval of fiduciary applications are set forth in 12 CFR 5.26, Fiduciary Powers, and the *Comptroller's Corporate Manual* booklet "Fiduciary Powers."

On September 10, 1984, the OCC first granted approval to exercise full fiduciary powers to a federal branch of a foreign bank operating in the United States. Approval was granted under 12 USC. 92a and in accordance with 12 CFR 5. A foreign bank must submit an application and obtain prior approval from the OCC before it exercises fiduciary powers at a federal branch. An application for fiduciary powers may be submitted at the time of filing an application for a federal branch license or at any subsequent date. Generally, federal branches have the same rights and privileges and are subject to the same duties, restrictions, penalties, liabilities, conditions, and limits as national banks doing business in the same location. See 12 CFR 28, International Banking Activities.

A bank that wishes to discontinue or voluntarily surrender its authority to exercise fiduciary powers must file with the OCC a certified copy of a board of directors' resolution that signifies its desire to do so in accordance with 12 CFR 9.17(a), Surrender or Revocation of Fiduciary Powers. A bank may be classified as inactive, or it may surrender its fiduciary powers altogether. In either case, the board of directors must arrange for a final audit of the fiduciary accounts. The OCC may conduct a closing investigation to determine that the bank has been discharged completely from its fiduciary obligations. The OCC will issue a written notice to the bank that it is no longer authorized to exercise fiduciary powers previously granted when the OCC is assured that the bank has been relieved of all fiduciary duties according to applicable law.

Pursuant to 12 USC 92a(k) and 12 CFR 9.17(b), the OCC may provide notice to a national bank of its intent to revoke the authority to exercise fiduciary powers. If the OCC determines that the bank has exercised its fiduciary powers unlawfully or unsoundly, the OCC may revoke those powers. The OCC may also revoke a bank's fiduciary powers if it has failed to exercise them for a period of five consecutive years. Refer to the *Comptroller's Corporate Manual* for specific information relating to the granting, surrender, and revocation of fiduciary powers.

Fiduciary activities are highly regulated. There are numerous laws and regulations intended to protect trust beneficiaries, retirement plan participants, corporate bondholders, and other types of investors. Professional corporate fiduciaries will generally be held to higher standards of care and prudence than other types of fiduciaries. These factors underscore the importance for a bank fiduciary to act solely in the best interest of its clients and to create an environment of high ethics and strong risk management processes.

National banks exercising fiduciary powers must comply with 12 CFR 9, Fiduciary Activities of National Banks; applicable fiduciary statutes enacted in each state in which a bank conducts such activities; and other applicable law. Examples of other fiduciary related laws and regulations include the Employee Retirement and Income Security Act of 1974 and 12 CFR 12, Recordkeeping and Confirmation Requirements for Securities Transactions.

12 CFR 9 was issued by the OCC to set forth standards that apply to the fiduciary activities of national banks granted fiduciary powers pursuant to 12 USC 92a. It applies to all national banks that act in a fiduciary capacity and all Federal branches of foreign banks to the same extent as it applies to national banks. A fiduciary account is defined in part 9 as "an account administered by a national bank acting in a fiduciary capacity." Fiduciary capacity means:

- A trustee, executor, administrator, registrar of stocks and bonds, transfer agent, guardian, assignee, receiver, or custodian under a uniform gifts to minors act;

- An investment adviser, if the bank receives a fee for its investment advice;

- Any capacity in which the bank possesses investment discretion on behalf of another; or

- Any other similar capacity that the OCC authorizes pursuant to 12 USC 92a.

International Fiduciary Services

Fiduciary powers may be exercised by a national bank through a foreign branch, by a subsidiary of the parent holding company, or by an Edge Act Corporation. In the case of a branch, 12 CFR 9 is applicable through the provisions of 12 USC 481 and 12 USC 1818(b)(1). If conducted through a holding company subsidiary or Edge Act Corporation, Regulation K of the Board of Governors of the Federal Reserve System (i.e., 12 CFR 211) applies. In these instances, 12 CFR 9 is normally used as a professional guide, although it could be applied indirectly by reason of 12 USC 1867 if the affiliate provides fiduciary services to a branch.

Foreign branches of national banks can engage in activities that are permissible for a national bank in the United States and are usual in connection with the business of banking in the country where it transacts business. Foreign branches of national banks are also subject to local fiduciary law in the jurisdiction where they transact business. See 12 CFR 28, International Banking Activities.

Other U.S. laws and regulations may or may not be applicable depending upon specific provisions and exemptions. Foreign branches of U.S. banks, for example, are exempt from the provisions of 12 CFR 12 and are not covered by Federal Deposit Insurance Corporation (FDIC) insurance. All types of foreign entities, on the other hand, can be included under various provisions of the Foreign Corrupt Practices Act of 1977.

Uniform Interagency Trust Rating System

The Uniform Interagency Trust Rating System (UITRS) was adopted on September 21, 1978, by the OCC, the FDIC, and the Federal Reserve Board, and in 1988 by the Federal Home Loan Bank Board, predecessor of the Office of Thrift Supervision. The UITRS helps the agencies to uniformly evaluate the fiduciary activities of financial institutions and to identify institutions requiring special attention.

The UITRS was revised in 1998 because of changes that had occurred in the fiduciary services industry and in supervisory policies and processes since the rating system was first adopted. Significant changes made to the rating system include the following:

- The numerical ratings were revised to conform to the language and tone of the definitions used by the Uniform Financial Institution Rating System.

- Descriptions of the component rating were reformatted and clarified.

- Increased emphasis was placed on the quality of risk management processes in each of the five rating components.

- The types of risk considered in assigning component ratings were explicitly identified.

The complete text of the revised UITRS will be included in a forthcoming revision of the "Bank Supervision Process" booklet of the *Comptroller's Handbook*.

Consumer Compliance

The activities of a corporate fiduciary are subject to compliance with applicable consumer laws and regulations unless specifically exempted. Please refer to the *Comptroller's Handbook* booklet "Consumer Compliance Examination" for specific information concerning the applicability of consumer compliance laws and regulation to the fiduciary activities of national banks.

Retail Securities Brokerage

National banks that engage in retail securities brokerage must comply with the guidelines established by the "Interagency Statement on Retail Sales of Nondeposit Investment Products," dated February 15, 1994 (interagency statement). The interagency statement establishes minimum operating standards for retail brokerage programs that help mitigate risks to both the financial institution and the consumer. The interagency statement covers retail nondeposit investment activities involving:

- Sales or recommendations to individuals made by bank employees or employees of affiliated or unaffiliated broker/dealers occurring on bank premises;

- Sales resulting from bank referrals of retail customers to an affiliated broker/dealer; and

- Sales resulting from bank referrals of retail customers to a third party when the bank receives a benefit for the referral.

The interagency statement applies only to banks and not broker/dealers. Broker/dealer firms that are members of the National Association of Securities Dealers, Inc. (NASD) and operate on bank premises must comply with NASD Rule 2350 Bank Broker/Dealer Rule. This rule mirrors many of the standards established in the interagency statement.

The interagency statement generally does not apply to fiduciary accounts administered by a depository institution primarily because fiduciary accounts are governed by other standards of care and prudence. However, the disclosures prescribed by the interagency statement should be provided for fiduciary accounts where the customer directs investments, such as self-directed individual retirement accounts.

Additional guidance is provided in the "Retail Nondeposit Investment Sales" section of the *Comptroller's Handbook for National Bank Examiners* and in OCC Bulletin 95-52, "Clarification of Interagency Statement Guidelines," dated September 22, 1995. OCC retail brokerage examinations focus on the risks created by the sales program and the adequacy and effectiveness of the bank's oversight and management of those risks.

Gramm-Leach-Bliley Act of 1999

Prior to the enactment of the Gramm-Leach-Bliley Act (GLBA), national banks engaged in securities brokerage activities were exempt from registering as a broker under the Securities Exchange Act of 1934 (Exchange Act). Under the GLBA, effective May 2001, banks lose this blanket exemption. If a bank engages in brokerage as defined in the Exchange Act, the bank will generally have to register as a broker. Once registered, these activities will be subject to primary regulation and oversight by the Securities and Exchange Commission (SEC). The SEC uses self-regulatory organizations, such as the NASD and the New York Stock Exchange, to assist in supervising broker/dealers.

Historically, national bank retail brokerage services have been provided directly by bank employees and/or through various types of arrangements with affiliated or unaffiliated third-party broker/dealers. Pursuant to GLBA, if a bank does not wish to register as a broker, a company's brokerage activities may be provided either in a separately registered brokerage subsidiary, through a holding company affiliate, or through arrangements with unaffiliated brokerage firms.

GLBA provides that a broker is "any person engaged in the business of effecting transactions in securities for the account of others." It also recognizes that certain banking activities involving securities transactions should not trigger broker registration requirements. Accordingly, the act lists several exceptions under which banks will not be considered to be a broker. Some of these exceptions are described below. A bank must meet the requirements of GLBA in order to qualify for these exceptions.

Third-party brokerage arrangements. A bank will not be considered to be a broker when it enters into a formal arrangement with an affiliated or unaffiliated broker/dealer under which the broker/dealer offers brokerage services on or off the bank's premises. Such arrangements must satisfy the following conditions:

- The broker/dealer must be clearly identified as the person performing the brokerage services.

- The brokerage activity must occur in a clearly marked area that is, to the extent practical, physically separate from the routine deposit-taking activities of the bank.

- Any materials used by the bank to advertise or promote generally the availability of brokerage services under the arrangement must clearly indicate that the brokerage services are provided by the broker/dealer, not the bank.

- Any materials used by the bank to advertise or promote generally the availability of brokerage services under the arrangement must be in compliance with federal securities laws before distribution.

- Bank employees (other than associated persons of a broker/dealer who are qualified pursuant to the rules of a self-regulatory organization) can only perform clerical or ministerial functions in connection with brokerage transactions, including scheduling appointments with the associated persons of a broker/dealer, except that bank employees may forward customer funds or securities and may describe in general terms the types of investment vehicles available from the bank and the broker/dealer under the arrangement.

- Bank employees may not receive incentive compensation for any brokerage transaction unless such employees are associated persons of a broker/dealer and are qualified pursuant to the rules of a self-regulatory organization. Bank employees may receive compensation for a referral of any customer if the compensation is a nominal one-time cash fee of a fixed dollar amount and the payment of the fee is not contingent on whether the referral results in a transaction.

- Broker/dealer services must be provided on a basis in which all customers that receive any services are fully disclosed to the broker/dealer.

- The bank may not carry a securities account of the customer except as permitted under the trust and safekeeping and custody sections of the act.

- The bank or broker/dealer must inform each customer that the brokerage services are provided by the broker/dealer and not the bank, and that the securities are not deposits or other obligations of the bank, are not guaranteed by the bank, and are not insured by the FDIC.

Trust Activities. A bank will not be considered to be a broker if it effects transactions in a trustee capacity, or effects transactions in a fiduciary capacity in its trust department or other department that is regularly examined by bank examiners for compliance with fiduciary principles and standards, and

- The bank is chiefly compensated for such transactions, consistent with fiduciary principles and standards, on the basis of an administrative or annual fee (payable on a monthly, quarterly, or other basis), a percentage of assets under management, a flat or capped per order processing fee equal to not more than the cost incurred by the bank in connection with executing securities transaction for trustee and fiduciary customers, or any combination of such fees; and

- The bank may not publicly solicit brokerage business, other than by advertising that it effects transactions in securities as part of its overall advertising of its general business.

Safekeeping and Custody Activities. A bank will not be considered to be a broker if, as part of its customary banking activities, the bank

- Provides safekeeping or custody services with respect to securities, including the exercise of warrants and other rights on behalf of customers;

- Facilitates the transfer of funds or securities, as custodian or a clearing agency, in connection with the clearance and settlement of its customers' securities transaction;

- Effects securities lending or borrowing transactions with or on behalf of customers as part of services provided to customers or invests cash collateral pledged in connection with such transactions;

- Holds securities pledged by a customer to another person or securities subject to purchase or resale agreements involving a customer, or facilitates the pledging or transfer of such securities by book entry or as otherwise provided under applicable law, if the bank maintains records separately identifying the securities and the customer; or

- Serves as a custodian or provider of other related administrative services to any individual retirement account, pension, retirement, profit sharing, bonus, thrift savings, incentive, or other similar benefit plan.

Stock Purchase Plans. A bank will not be considered to be a broker if it provides stocks transfer agency services for the following types of stock purchase plans:

- *Employee Benefit Plans.* This exception includes the securities of an issuer as part of any pension, retirement, profit-sharing, bonus, thrift, savings, incentive, or other similar benefit plan for the employees of that issuer or its affiliates. To qualify for the exception, the bank cannot solicit transactions or provide investment advice with respect to the purchase or sale of securities in connection with the plan.

- *Dividend Reinvestment Plans.* This exception includes the securities of an issuer as part of that issuer's dividend reinvestment plan if

  - The bank does not solicit transactions or provide investment advice with respect to the purchase or sale of securities in connection with the plan, and

  - The bank does not net shareholders' buy and sell orders, other than for programs for odd-lot holders or plans registered with the SEC.

- *Issuer Plans.* This exception includes securities of an issuer as part of a plan or program for the purchase or sale of that issuer's shares if

  - The bank does not solicit transactions or provide investment advice with respect to the purchase or sale of securities in connection with the plan or program, and

  - The bank does not net shareholders' buy and sell orders, other than for programs for odd-lot holders or plans registered with the SEC.

Sweep Accounts. A bank will not be considered to be a broker if the bank effects transactions as part of a program for the investment or reinvestment of deposit funds into any no-load, open-end management investment company registered under the Investment Company Act of 1940 that holds itself out as a money market fund.

De Minimus Exception. A bank will not be considered to be a broker if the bank does not effect more than 500 transactions in securities in any calendar year (other than in transactions referred to in previous exceptions), and such transactions are not effected by an employee of the bank who is also an employee of a broker/dealer.

The exceptions granted to a bank under the "Trust Activities," "Safekeeping and Custody Activities," and "Stock Purchase Plans" sections will not apply unless

- The bank directs such trades to a registered broker/dealer for execution;

- The trade is a cross trade or other substantially similar trade of a security that (1) is made by the bank or between the bank and an affiliated fiduciary and (2) is not in contravention of fiduciary principles established under applicable federal or state law; or

- The trade is conducted in some other manner permitted under the rules, regulations, or orders as the SEC may prescribe or issue.

Investment Company Services

A bank that provides financial services to registered investment companies may be subject to any applicable federal securities laws that govern investment companies. The Investment Company Act of 1940 (ICA) and the Investment Advisers Act of 1940 (IAA) are the primary statutes controlling the activities of investment companies and their associated service providers. These statutes establish a variety of registration, reporting, and regulatory requirements on investment companies and investment advisers. The SEC is responsible for the administration, regulation, and enforcement of these statutes.

Prior to the enactment of GLBA, banks were exempt from investment adviser registration under the IAA. As a result of this exemption, many banks provided investment advisory services through unregistered internal bank divisions. Other banks made strategic decisions to provide these services through registered investment advisory bank subsidiaries or holding company affiliates. GLBA amended the IAA to require a bank to register with the SEC as an investment adviser if the bank provides investment advisory services to a registered investment company. All other investment advisory activities conducted in the bank, including investment advisory activities involving collective investment funds and other unregistered investment funds (such as private equity funds) are still exempt from federal investment adviser registration requirements.

Banks that are required to register their investment advisory services have four organizational methods available to them:

- The bank may register itself as an investment adviser.
- The bank may register a "separately identifiable department or division" (SIDD) of the bank that performs the advisory services.
- The bank may register a subsidiary that performs the advisory services.
- A holding company subsidiary or other affiliate that performs the advisory services can be registered.

Investment adviser registration will subject the bank's investment advisory activities to regulation by the SEC under the IAA. While a bank must register its advisory function to the extent it advises a registered investment company, it may choose to consolidate some or all of its investment advisory activities in the registered entity. The investment advisory activities included in the registered investment adviser must adhere to the IAA. The IAA and the rules promulgated under the IAA regulate advertising, solicitation, and receipt of performance fees by registered investment advisers. Investment adviser registration requires the adviser to, among other things,

- Establish procedures to prevent the misuse of nonpublic information;

- Maintain certain books and records, and submit periodic information reports to the SEC;

- Supervise investment advisory firm employees;

- Comply with the general anti-fraud provisions of the federal securities laws; and

- Become statutorily disqualified from performing certain services for a mutual fund if the adviser violates the law.

Risks

National banks that engage in asset management activities operate within a broad and complex risk environment. The most obvious risks are created by or arise out of specific client agreements, legal documents, investment portfolio strategies, laws and regulations, court rulings, and other recognized fiduciary principles. Other risks, which are more subtle but as potentially damaging, arise from the manner in which an institution markets itself, the quality and integrity of the individuals it employs, and the type of leadership and strategic direction provided by its board of directors and senior management.

The potential for loss, either through direct expense charges or from loss of clients, arises when a bank fails to fulfill its fiduciary and contractual responsibilities to customers, shareholders, and regulatory authorities. Significant breaches of fiduciary and contractual responsibilities can result in financial losses, damage a bank's reputation, and impair its ability to achieve its strategic goals and objectives.

Asset management activities can expose the bank to the potential for financial loss through litigation, fraud, theft, lost business, and wasted capital from failed strategic initiatives. Losses from asset management activities typically result from inadequate internal controls, weak risk management systems, inadequate training, or deficient board and management oversight. Several banks have experienced significant, highly publicized losses relating to asset management (although such losses are not the norm). Maintaining a good reputation and positive public image is vital to a successful asset management business.

The earnings and capital of banks with significant reliance on asset management revenues may be adversely affected when financial markets experience a significant and sustained downturn. Asset management revenues are dependent on transaction volumes and market values of assets under management and may decline during periods of adverse market movements.

Within the framework of the OCC's risk assessment system, national banks that provide asset management products and services are directly exposed to **transaction, compliance, strategic, and reputation** risks. In addition, a national bank as fiduciary has indirect exposure to **credit, interest rate, liquidity, and price** risks because these risks are inherent in the financial instruments that it holds and in the portfolios that it manages or advises for its customers. A failure to prudently manage these risks at the account level can increase a bank's level of transaction, compliance, strategic, and reputation risk.

An institution such as a special purpose trust bank may have direct exposure to **liquidity, interest rate, price**, and, possibly, **credit** risks. Refer to OCC Bulletin 2000-26, "Supervision of National Trust Banks," for more information on financial risks that affect trust banks. In addition, significant losses and damaged reputation from asset management activities could directly affect any institution's liquidity position by impairing its access to capital markets, increasing its cost of funds, and leading to unanticipated loss of deposits and capital sources.

Transaction Risk

Transaction risk exists in all types of products and services. A characteristic of asset management is a high volume of various types of transactions, particularly securities transactions. The processing of securities transactions must be accurately and timely executed and recorded for each account. Income from investments must be credited to the accounts and then properly disbursed to the account holders. Account statements and reports must be generated to the interested parties, including account holders, courts, and federal agencies. Many banks outsource transaction processing and financial record keeping to third-party vendors. Some examples of issues that could raise an institution's level of transaction risk are

- Deficient information processing, accounting, reconcilement, and reporting systems in relation to transaction volume and complexity.

- Deficient operating processes and internal controls over information systems and accounting records, particularly during system conversions.

- Inadequate disaster contingency planning for information systems.

- Failure to effectively manage third-party vendors.

Compliance Risk

Compliance risk is a significant factor in the overall risk framework of asset management activities. It is not limited to simply compliance with laws and regulations; it encompasses sound fiduciary principles, prudent ethical standards, client documents, internal policies and procedures, and other contractual obligations. Some examples of issues that could raise an institution's level of compliance risk are

- Deficient account acceptance and review processes.

- Deficiencies in the ethical culture and expertise of management and supporting personnel.

- Weak internal compliance systems and training programs.

- Failure to use legal counsel effectively.

Strategic Risk

Strategic risk involves more than an analysis of the strategic plan for asset management activities. It relates to how asset management strategies, business plans, systems, and implementation processes affect a bank's franchise value, as well as how management analyzes external factors that affect the strategic direction of a bank. The resources needed to carry out asset management strategies are both tangible and intangible. They include communication channels, operating systems, delivery networks, and managerial capacities and capabilities. Some examples of issues that could raise an institution's level of strategic risk are

- Failure to adopt and implement an asset management strategic planning process.

- Failure to provide adequate financial, technological, and human resources to asset management business lines and control functions.

- Weaknesses in the administration of acquisitions, mergers, and alliances.

Reputation Risk

The assessment of reputation risk recognizes the potential impact of public opinion on a company's franchise value. Asset management activities are likely to produce a high level of reputation risk. As a company's vulnerability to public reaction increases, its ability to offer innovative products and services may be affected. An institution's reputation is enhanced through competitive investment performance, state-of-the-art products and services, high-quality customer service, and compliance with applicable law. Some examples of issues that could raise an institution's level of reputation risk are

- Lack of a strong and enforced ethical culture and risk control environment.

- Lack of a clearly defined and consistently applied investment management philosophy.

- Deficiencies in the integration of sales-oriented businesses with the responsibilities associated with fiduciary relationships.

- Marginal or poor customer service and product performance.

- Adverse regulatory enforcement actions.

- Liability for damages or restitution as a result of litigation.

Many larger banks provide asset management products and services that are more sophisticated and global in nature, such as the use of financial derivatives and other alternative investment classes. These activities create diverse and complex risks that require an enhanced level of assessment, control, and monitoring. But regardless of its size, a bank that provides asset management products and services must be able to understand and manage the risks.

Risk Management

The acceptance of risk is an inevitable part of providing asset management products and services, and risk management is an important responsibility of a national bank engaging in these activities. Sound risk management is especially critical in banks undergoing mergers and consolidations. Strong risk controls and sophisticated monitoring systems are essential in large, diversified companies to ensure effective risk management across a company's entire organizational framework.

Risk management represents a variety of challenges for national banks offering asset management services. This is partly because it is difficult to develop relevant analytical and statistical risk measures for many asset management lines of business. In addition, a purely analytical system may not be sufficient to assess and monitor all risks in this business. Consequently, risk management objectives and functions for asset management may vary significantly between banks.

Because market conditions, risk strategies, and organizational structures vary, there is no single risk management system that works for all companies. Each bank should establish a risk management program suitable for its own needs and circumstances. The formality of the process should be commensurate with the complexity of the organization's structure and operations. An effective risk management system ensures that a comprehensive risk profile of a bank's asset management activities is developed and maintained by supervising, assessing, controlling, and monitoring the many different risks associated with asset management products and services.

Risk Supervision

The board of directors and senior management must be committed to risk management for processes to be effective. Acknowledged acceptance and oversight of the risk management process by the board and senior management is important. Institutions that have been successful in prudent risk taking have a corporate culture that balances risk controls and business initiatives. Directors must recognize their responsibility to provide proper oversight of asset management activities, and the official records of the board should clearly reflect the proper discharge of that responsibility.

Directors must understand the asset management business, how asset management activities affect the bank's position and reputation, the bank's regulatory environment, and other external market factors. The board must recognize and understand existing risks and risks that may arise from new business initiatives, including risks that originate in bank and nonbank subsidiaries and affiliates, such as investment advisory and brokerage companies.

The board is ultimately responsible for any financial loss or reduction in shareholder value suffered by the bank. Because of the fiduciary nature of many asset management activities and the standards to which fiduciaries are generally held, directors should use prudence in their oversight of these activities to ensure that applicable fiduciary laws and principles are not violated. If, through their failure to exercise prudent oversight, losses accrue to account principals, beneficiaries, or the bank, directors can be held liable for such losses in an action for damages.

Key responsibilities of the board and senior management relating to asset management activities include the following:

- **Establish the strategic direction, risk tolerance standards, and ethical culture for asset management activities.**

- **Adopt and implement an adequate and effective risk management system.**

- **Monitor the implementation of asset management risk-taking strategies and the adequacy and effectiveness of the risk management system in achieving the company's strategic goals and financial objectives.**

The board of directors and senior management should establish a supervisory environment that communicates their commitment to risk management and a sound internal control system. They must establish and guide the strategic direction for asset management activities by approving strategic and financial operating plans. The goal is to create a risk management culture that promotes strong ethics and an environment of responsibility and accountability that is fully accepted within the banking organization.

It is the responsibility of senior management to ensure the development and implementation of an adequate and effective risk management system composed of risk assessment, control, and monitoring processes. Business line management is responsible for day-to-day risk assessment and implementing appropriate risk controls and monitoring systems. To enhance risk management capabilities, the organization should use common risk terminology. Using the same risk terminology facilitates communication across functions, divisions, departments, and business units, as well as vertically among management levels.

In large banks, the asset management organization may have a separate risk management function that operates under the umbrella of the bank's corporate-wide risk management organization. The corporate organization may consist of senior executives, line managers, compliance, audit, legal, operations, human resources, information systems, and product development units that work together under the administration of a board-designated risk management committee.

It is critical that the board, its designated committees, and senior management provide effective oversight and monitoring of asset management activities. This responsibility may be assisted through the activities of other risk monitoring functions such as risk management, audit, and compliance groups, but the ultimate responsibility and liability rests with the board and senior management.

Risk Assessment

The evolution and growth of the asset management business in national banks have made risk assessment more complex and challenging. The diversity and complexity of the business and the speed and volume at which transactions occur heighten the need for an effective risk assessment process that is integrated with a bank's overall risk assessment system. The process of risk assessment includes identifying, estimating, and evaluating all risks associated with asset management and grouping them into appropriate risk categories. When risks of certain activities cannot be realistically estimated, management must be able to reasonably assess, control, and monitor the impact such activities may have on a bank's strategic plan and financial performance.

Management should assess risks by evaluating the quality and performance of existing products and services and the adequacy and effectiveness of risk management processes. Other factors management should consider are the regulatory, economic, and political environment in which asset management services are provided and the company's ability to achieve its strategic objectives and financial goals for this business. The level of risk and the quality of risk management processes should be considered when making decisions on product and service pricing, new business proposals, employee compensation, and the amount of capital needed to adequately support asset management activities.

Risk Control

Risk controls are essential to risk management. The types and sophistication of control processes should be consistent with the risk tolerance standards established by the board of directors and senior management. A process should be implemented for tracking and reporting risk exposures to monitor whether the bank is in compliance with risk tolerance standards and whether its asset management businesses are meeting financial goals and objectives.

Strategic planning. Sound strategic planning is a cornerstone of effective risk control, and one of the board's primary responsibilities is to establish and guide the bank's strategic direction. The increasing competition in the delivery of financial products and services and the dynamic nature of the industry demand continuous strategic planning and monitoring. The board is responsible for approving the bank's strategic asset management goals and objectives and providing the necessary managerial, financial, technological, and organizational resources to achieve those goals and objectives.

Strategic planning for asset management activities should be a part of a bank's overall strategic planning process and should usually be the joint responsibility of senior and business line management. Management should use the strategic plan adopted by the board as the direction for developing long- and short-term business plans, policies, internal controls, staffing, training, and management information systems for asset management lines of business. It is also important for management to have effective systems in place to communicate strategic objectives and strategies so that all levels of the organization understand and support them.

The responsibility for assessing the adequacy of capital to support asset management activities rests with the board and senior management and should be a continuous part of the strategic planning process. The amount of capital necessary to support these activities should be reflective of, and appropriate for, the quantity of risk and the quality of risk management systems within the institution.

Risk culture and ethical environment. The board of directors and senior management should establish an appropriate risk culture and promote an ethical environment. Most institutions in this business have adopted a code of ethics and established specific standards of conduct for its employees' internal and external activities. To be effective tools of risk management, such standards should be clearly communicated (to reduce the likelihood of misinterpretation and misunderstandings) and properly enforced.

Organization. The board of directors and senior management should adopt an appropriate organizational structure for asset management activities. An integrated organizational framework that depicts key managerial authorities, responsibilities, and risk control processes down to operational levels must underpin the risk management system.

The organization should be designed to promote efficient and effective operations. Bank records should clearly define organizational relationships, responsibilities, and control processes. Reporting lines should identify key personnel accountable for risk management oversight. The structure of asset management activities should be set forth in bylaws, board resolutions, or written management plans adopted by the board or its designated committee.

The board may establish formal committees to supervise asset management activities. Committee membership and responsibilities should be clearly established, communicated, and periodically reviewed by the board and senior management. Committees should meet regularly and report to the board of directors. Significant actions taken by committees should be recorded in committee minutes, or in a similar record when performed by designated persons. Records should be reviewed, or be available for inspection, by the board. Board minutes should note such review, or that such records are available to directors for review.

The organizational structure should facilitate the implementation of a sound internal control system, including a procedure for management's review of actions taken by all personnel. Communication processes should be in place that keep senior management informed of the effectiveness of risk management processes and inform personnel of the bank's objectives, risk tolerance standards, products and services, and policies and procedures. Employees should be provided relevant and timely information on the institution's operating environment, such as trends in the financial markets or changes in applicable statutory and regulatory standards.

The board should make a periodic formal assessment of the organization and administration of asset management activities. As asset management activities expand into the delivery of new and more complex financial products and services, the bank may need rapid and sometimes dramatic organizational changes. The introduction of integrated marketing and delivery systems, such as private banking and the Internet, create new and challenging risks for a board and its management team. Directors should ensure that organizational changes do not hinder the bank's ability to fulfill its fiduciary responsibilities and comply with applicable law.

Management and personnel practices. The board and senior management are responsible for the selection and compensation of managers. Effective risk management requires experienced and competent managers and supporting staff. Managers must understand and support the bank s mission, values, policies, and processes; supporting staff should be experienced, well trained, and adequate in number to administer asset management activities in a safe and sound manner.

Management should have policies and procedures for personnel recruitment, training, performance evaluation, and salary administration. Lines of authority, duties, and responsibilities should be clearly defined and communicated to all personnel. Because of rapid and frequent changes in products, customers, markets, and technology, continuing education programs are very important in this business. A comprehensive training program implemented and supported by management is essential.

Policies. The board, or its designated committee(s), should adopt asset management policies that promote sound risk management processes.

Policies should be developed and approved in a manner the board deems most appropriate for the bank. Policies should specifically address the bank's unique goals and objectives, risk tolerance standards, risk management processes, internal control systems, and compliance with applicable law. Policy guidelines relating to fiduciary activities are included in 12 CFR 9.5, Policies and procedures, and 12 CFR 12.7, Securities Trading Policies and Procedures.

The coverage and detail in policies will vary among banks depending on their complexity and organizational framework. But policies should address significant lines of business and support functions, include clear standards of performance, and be effectively communicated to all levels of the asset management organization. The policy should contain product and service pricing guidelines and address fee concessions, if applicable. Refer to the "Conflicts of Interest" booklet of the *Comptroller's Handbook* for additional information on OCC policy relating to fee concessions.

The board, or its designated committee, should review asset management policies at least annually and revise them when significant changes occur in risk strategies, resources, activities, or operating environment. Policies and procedures for new products and services should be in place before the products and services are sold to ensure proper implementation. Policies should be applied consistently throughout the organization.

Internal control systems. Effective internal control is the foundation for the safe and sound operation of a banking institution, including asset management activities. The board of directors and senior management are responsible for establishing and maintaining effective control functions commensurate with the institution's asset management goals and objectives, risk tolerance standards, complexity of operations, and other regulatory and environmental factors.

The board, or its designated committee(s), should adopt the policies that establish the internal control system for asset management activities and ensure that management is appropriately administering the internal control system. The internal control system should facilitate risk management strategies and be adequately supported by audit and compliance programs, staffing, information systems and communication processes. Refer to the "Internal Control" booklet of the *Comptroller's Handbook* for additional information about internal controls.

Product development and marketing. New products and services provide the opportunity to improve performance and diversify risk by developing additional revenue streams and establishing new client relationships. The competitive environment in which banks compete disposes them to introduce new financial products and services. A bank's ability to respond to market changes and customer demands will determine its long-term competitiveness and financial success. Management must be able to respond to the risks that may arise from changing business conditions or the introduction of new products and services.

The board of directors should require management to assess the risks and potential returns of proposed products and services and establish appropriate systems for their development and distribution. New products and services frequently require different pricing, processing, accounting, and risk measurement systems. Management and the board must ensure that the bank has adequate knowledge, staff, technology, and financial resources to accommodate the activity. Furthermore, plans to enter new markets or sell new products should take into account the cost of establishing appropriate controls, as well as attracting professional staff with the necessary expertise.

For new and existing products and services, a uniform product assessment process should be part of the overall risk management program. The goal of this process should be to ensure that all significant risks are addressed. The new product approval process should include appropriate review and documentation processes by risk management, operations, accounting, legal, audit and business line management. Proposed products, services, and distribution channels should be evaluated and tested before full distribution begins. Depending on the magnitude of the new product or service and its impact on the bank's risk profile, senior management, and in some cases the board, should provide the final approval.

Vendor Management. National banks increasingly use third-party vendors to perform various administrative, operational, and investment advisory services. The OCC encourages national banks to use third-party vendors that provide legitimate and safe opportunities to enhance product offerings, improve earnings, and diversify operations. The OCC expects national banks to have an effective process for managing third-party service arrangements involving asset management products and services.

Before entering into a major relationship with a third-party vendor, a national bank should establish a comprehensive program for managing the relationship. Such programs should be documented and include front-end management planning and appropriate due diligence for vendor selection and performance monitoring. OCC Advisory Letter 2000-9, "Third-Party Risk," provides guidance for establishing an effective vendor management program.

Information systems and technology application. Effective risk control is dependent on accurate, timely, reliable, and relevant information processing and reporting systems. The board and senior management must receive adequate information on the performance of asset management activities to properly fulfill their responsibilities. Rapid advancements in information technology create new risk and control issues that affect the asset management activities of national banks. The board should ensure that management properly considers the impact of emerging technologies on product distribution channels, information systems, staffing, training, and any other relevant factor.

Information security is critical and should be a strategic objective of any bank. A bank should establish an information security program tailored to its size and the nature and scope of its operations. The OCC is developing standards for national bank information security programs that will be included in the appendix to 12 CFR 30, Safety and Soundness Standards.

A bank's information security program should include asset management lines of business. Policies should be in writing and communicated to all personnel and other authorized users of asset management information systems. Controls should be in place to minimize the vulnerability of all information to errors, misuse, and loss. The level of control should be commensurate with the degree of exposure and the impact of potential losses on the institution, including dollar loss, competitive disadvantage, damaged reputation, improper disclosure, lawsuits, or regulatory sanctions.

A contingency and business resumption plan for asset management activities is a key element of effective information security systems. The board and management are responsible for establishing policies, procedures, and monitoring processes to ensure effective business resumption, contingency planning, and testing. Contingency plans should address all critical functions and operations of asset management and should be coordinated with the bank's overall contingency planning process. Plans should be reviewed at least annually by the board and senior management.

Because of the considerable investment in technology that is required to deliver competitive asset management products and services, many institutions purchase information technology rather than develop their own internal systems. For example, many asset management organizations do not develop in-house accounting and transaction-processing systems, but instead contract with third-party service providers. This market is dominated by relatively few vendors. The choice between internal development and maintenance or contracting with third-party vendors depends on the size and nature of the products and services provided, the availability of skilled personnel, and the financial resources of the institution.

Whatever the source of information systems, the board and management must exercise a proper level of control and oversight to appropriately fulfill their fiduciary duties. Vendor contracts should be thoroughly reviewed by legal counsel to ensure that they include appropriate indemnification and recourse language. In addition, contracts should contain specific language recognizing the authority of the institution's functional regulator to conduct reviews of third-party vendors as part of their overall supervisory activities.

Risk Monitoring

The board of directors, its designated committees, and senior management should regularly monitor and evaluate the types and levels of asset management risk and the adequacy and effectiveness of risk management processes. Well-designed monitoring processes will assist the board in evaluating management's performance in achieving the bank's strategic and financial objectives for asset management. The board must determine whether management is appropriately implementing its strategic directives and policy guidance and managing risk positions, control systems, and policy exceptions in an effective manner. Monitoring reports should be frequent, timely, accurate, and useful.

The following sections describe various types of risk monitoring functions used by national banks. There is no standard organizational structure for risk monitoring and in many banks these functions may be combined or have significant overlapping responsibilities. For example, a bank may have a risk management organization that combines the supervision of risk managers with audit, compliance, legal, and financial reporting functions. The manner in which risk monitoring processes are administered and operated is dependent on the needs of the individual organization.

Risk management function. As previously noted, larger banks may have established a corporate-wide, risk management function that includes asset management lines of business. The administration and operation of this function may be independent from business lines and relied upon by the board to provide a continuous, objective assessment of risk and risk management processes. Smaller banks may not have a separate risk management function or unit dedicated to asset management. They may instead rely on other risk management and internal control processes suited to their needs and resources. Appendix A of this booklet presents general guidelines for operating a risk management function.

Whatever the organizational framework, the risk management function should be supervised and staffed with sufficient expertise and resources. In some banks, this may require support from other risk managers or bank personnel outside the asset management risk group who possess specialized product knowledge and technical and analytical risk management skills.

Compliance program. A compliance program can play a central role in monitoring certain risks associated with asset management activities. Compliance with laws, regulations, internal policies and control processes, customer account documents, and sound fiduciary principles is essential to any fiduciary. Ensuring such compliance is a key responsibility of a board of directors. Directors and management must recognize the scope and implications of applicable law and establish a compliance program that protects the bank from adverse litigation, increased regulatory oversight, and damage to its reputation. The compliance management system must be periodically reviewed for relevance, effectiveness, and appropriate follow-up.

Asset management organizations take different approaches to compliance programs. For large organizations with complex services and structures, the OCC strongly encourages formalized compliance programs with frequent compliance monitoring. Less formalized programs may be appropriate for smaller organizations. All programs, however, should make compliance an integral part of each employee's job. Effective compliance programs have common elements that include

- A strong commitment from the board and senior management;

- A formalized program coordinated by a designated compliance officer that includes periodic testing and validation processes;

- Responsibility and accountability from line management;

- Effective communication systems;

- Comprehensive training programs; and

- Timely reporting and follow-up processes.

The active involvement of senior management with the support of the board of directors generally ensures that compliance is accorded high priority within the organization. Management's and the board's commitment should be communicated to all employees so they understand their obligation to perform their duties in compliance with applicable law and internal policies. In this same manner, accountability for compliance is appropriately placed on line management. Responsibility for compliance duties should be clearly established in individual job descriptions and should be an element in performance evaluations.

The compliance program should be in all respects a management tool; as such, it may not require the amount of independence that an audit unit must have. If independence is not practical, staff members who are not directly involved in the activities they are monitoring should perform compliance monitoring. Management should have a monitoring system in place to evaluate the effectiveness of its compliance program. Management should also be accountable to the board for compliance risk and the proper administration of the compliance program.

Employees must have a working knowledge of laws and regulations that apply to their job. Larger organizations often accomplish this through the employment of a full- or part-time compliance officer, who is responsible for providing compliance training to other personnel. Smaller departments may achieve a workable system without designating a separate compliance officer. Whatever system is used, it must provide timely, relevant, and accurate compliance information to appropriate personnel.

Control self-assessments. In control self-assessments, business units assume the primary responsibility for broadly identifying key business and operational risks. Periodically these units formally evaluate existing control systems and establish new ones, as necessary. Such control systems include policies and operating procedures. Self-assessments help managers improve their ability to manage risk by strengthening their understanding of risks that directly affect their areas of responsibility. The process forces self-discipline and places accountability in the areas where risk is actually taken and managed.

Because business line managers administer control self-assessment reviews, the reports may not be totally objective. Directors, senior management, and other risk managers should, therefore, be cautious when reviewing the results of these assessments and should ensure that a process is in place to validate the integrity and reliability of the self-assessment program.

Audit. A well-designed and executed audit program is essential to risk management and internal control as banks expand into new products, services, and technologies, including those related to asset management. An effective audit program provides the board of directors and senior management with an independent assessment of the efficiency and effectiveness of an organization's internal control system. When properly structured and implemented, the audit function provides important information about asset management risk levels and the adequacy and effectiveness of control systems that can help management take appropriate and timely corrective action.

The audit requirements for fiduciary activities are established by 12 CFR 9, Fiduciary Activities of National Banks, and are included in the "Internal and External Audits" booklet of the *Comptroller's Handbook*. 12 CFR 9.9 requires national banks with fiduciary powers to perform a "suitable audit" of all significant fiduciary activities during each calendar year. Alternatively, a national bank may adopt a continuous audit system that reviews significant fiduciary activities according to an appropriate assessment of risk.

The OCC does not specifically define what comprises a "suitable audit." Because the scope and coverage of fiduciary audits should be based on an assessment of risk, it is not appropriate for the OCC to precisely define minimum audit standards for fiduciary audits. The determination of a suitable audit for fiduciary activities is the responsibility of the board of directors or its designated committee. This determination should be based on an appropriate assessment of fiduciary business risk and internal control systems, and will be reviewed for adequacy and effectiveness by the OCC.

The FFIEC's "Interagency Policy Statement on the Internal Audit Function and Its Outsourcing" provides additional guidance on the characteristics of an effective internal audit function, and can be applied to the standards established for fiduciary audits in 12 CFR 9. The policy statement affirms that internal audit programs should be based on a risk assessment methodology that documents the institution's significant business activities and their associated risks. The frequency and extent of the internal audit review and testing should be consistent with the nature, complexity, and risk of the institution's financial activities. Audit programs should describe the objectives of specific audit activities and list the procedures that will be performed during the process.

Please refer to the "Internal and External Audits" booklet of the *Comptroller's Handbook* for additional information on fiduciary audits.

Management information systems (MIS). Asset management MIS should have clearly defined policies, procedures, practices, and standards, and provide the board and management with the necessary information tools to effectively supervise these activities. Information system technology must be adequate to support planned growth objectives, strategic acquisitions, and changes in business strategies.

The type, amount, and timing of information provided in board and management reports should be commensurate with the risk characteristics of the activities. Accurate, relevant, consistent, complete, and timely information is vital to support risk management decisions at all levels of the asset management organization. Management decisions based upon ineffective, inaccurate, or incomplete MIS may significantly increase risk. The "Management Information Systems" booklet of *the Comptroller's Handbook* should be referred to for additional guidance.

Financial performance reviews. The board, or its designated committees, and senior management should periodically monitor the financial performance of asset management activities. Information to consider includes the organization's success in achieving strategic goals and objectives; the quantity, quality, and volatility of earnings in relation to established risk tolerance standards; the performance of new products and services; and key financial performance measurement tools used by management. The financial reviews should assess the adequacy of capital allocated to support the various business lines; if necessary, appropriate adjustments to capital should be made. The board, or its designated committees, should review and approve recommended changes to asset management business plans prior to their implementation.

Regardless of how financial performance is measured and reported, management should strive to operate asset management activities in a profitable manner. Management must be sufficiently informed about financial performance and risk levels in order to make appropriate financial decisions. A well-designed financial reporting system specific to asset management products and services can provide much of the critical information necessary for sound financial decisions and effective risk management.

OCC Supervisory Processes

Supervision by Risk

The policies and processes that distinguish supervision by risk are fully described in the "Bank Supervision Process" booklet of the *Comptroller's Handbook*. The OCC's philosophy for supervising national banks focuses on the evaluation of risk and the promotion of sound risk management systems. This philosophy is applied to all banking activities, including asset management. The OCC's supervision of asset management activities in national banks is designed to:

- Continually assess the risks associated with current and planned asset management activities, including material risks originating in subsidiaries and affiliates that are subject to the primary supervision of another regulator.

- Evaluate the adequacy and effectiveness of risk management systems, including audit programs and internal controls, using periodic validation through transaction testing.

- Ensure adherence to safe and sound banking practices and compliance with applicable laws and regulations, subject to appropriate reliance on any functional regulator of particular activities.

- Communicate findings, recommendations, and requirements to bank management and directors in a clear and timely manner.

- Obtain informal or formal commitments to correct significant deficiencies in a timely manner and verify that such deficiencies have been appropriately corrected.

- Use OCC resources efficiently and effectively by allocating greater resources to the areas of asset management that pose the highest risk.

Assessing Risk

The OCC has established a three-part supervisory structure that integrates risk-based supervision into all aspects of the supervisory process. The three components are core knowledge, core assessment, and expanded examination procedures. These components are designed to ensure that risks are properly assessed and evaluated across the entire organization, regardless of its size, the diversity of its operations, or the existence of subsidiaries and affiliates. Each significant asset management activity is assessed and evaluated using the processes established by these components. For a complete description of these components, please refer to the "Bank Supervision Process," the "Large Bank Supervision," and the "Community Bank Supervision" booklets of the *Comptroller's Handbook*.

The OCC maintains a core knowledge database that contains information about the asset management activities of each national banking company. Data elements of the core knowledge database capture the bank's organization, management, products and services, and certain financial information. The database provides a foundation for risk assessment and helps examiners determine when supervisory activities should be expanded beyond the core assessment standards (CAS).

The CAS are designed to guide examiners in reaching conclusions regarding risks, risk management, and applicable regulatory rating systems. The standards establish the minimum conclusions that examiners must reach during an institution's supervisory cycle. By using these standards, examiners can assess risk within significant asset management activities. When risk is high or complex, examiners may expand the CAS procedures to include the expanded procedures in the applicable asset management booklet of the *Comptroller's Handbook*. The expanded examination procedures contain detailed guidance that explains how to examine specific activities or products that warrant extra attention.

The CAS complement the OCC's risk assessment system (RAS). The RAS documents examiners' assessments of the quantity of risk, the quality of risk management, the level of supervisory concern (measured as aggregate risk), and the direction of expected change. Together, the CAS and RAS provide the OCC with appropriate guidelines to measure and assess existing and emerging asset management risks for all banks, regardless of size and complexity. For a complete discussion of the RAS, please refer to the "Large Bank Supervision" booklet of the *Comptroller's Handbook.*

The OCC's risk-oriented approach to supervision does not attempt to prevent risk, but tries to ensure that banks understand and control the risks they assume. Asset management risk controls may be different because of the unique nature of the business, but the manner in which risk is defined, identified, measured and evaluated is uniform across the OCC.

Supervision Processes

The OCC continually supervises asset management activities. The supervisory framework includes the establishment of objectives, examination activities, and communication processes designed to effectively evaluate risk and promote sound risk management processes. The supervisory planning process for each institution involves a thorough assessment of current and anticipated asset management risks. Based on that assessment, an appropriate supervisory strategy is established and implemented.

Individual bank supervisory strategies are developed through coordination by examiners-in-charge or portfolio managers with assigned asset management examiners. The strategies are then reviewed and approved by the appropriate supervisory office. The supervisory strategy includes the OCC's objectives, activities, and work plans for significant asset management activities and becomes a part of the bank's overall supervisory strategy. Objectives define the goals of supervision for each bank based on its risk profile and other appropriate statutory or agency standards. Activities are the steps designed to achieve the supervisory objectives. The scope of activities must be consistent with supervisory objectives and ensure that the CAS, RAS, and UITRS are completed and updated. Work plans should outline the scope, timing, and resources needed to accomplish supervisory objectives and activities relating to asset management.

OCC examiners who supervise asset management activities have a broad range of specialized skills and expertise in the areas of fiduciary, investment management, and retail brokerage lines of business. To help ensure high-quality and consistent supervision, they spend most of their time, and in many cases all of it, supervising asset management activities. Assignments are periodically rotated to ensure an objective and fresh supervisory perspective.

The OCC has divided banks into two groups — large banks and community banks — as described in the "Bank Supervision Process" booklet of the *Comptroller's Handbook*. The definitions and supervisory policies and procedures for each category are in the "Large Bank Supervision" and "Community Bank Supervision" booklets of the *Comptroller's Handbook.*

These policies and processes should be consistently applied to significant asset management activities.

Large Bank Supervision

The largest banks are assigned to large bank deputy comptrollers in Washington, D.C. Other large banks are assigned to assistant deputy comptrollers in the OCC's district offices. The large bank program also assesses the risks to the bank posed by related entities, to the extent necessary to reach conclusions about the consolidated organization. For asset management activities, this assessment may involve investment company, investment advisory, retail brokerage, and investment banking affiliates and subsidiaries. Refer to the "Bank Supervision Process" booklet for information on supervising functionally regulated entities.

The supervision process in large banks is continuous. This is accomplished through a combination of periodic on-site and off-site supervisory activities. The supervisory cycle for asset management examination activities in large banks is 12 months. The scheduling of targeted asset management examinations in large banks during the supervisory cycle is based on an appropriate evaluation of risk and is part of a bank's consolidated supervisory strategy. Quarterly monitoring and reporting processes are another key component of the overall supervisory process. Refer to the "Bank Supervision Process" booklet of the *Comptroller's Handbook* for specific information on asset management supervisory cycles and examination scheduling policies.

Large bank CAS are structured according to the nine risk categories in the RAS, internal controls, and the CAMELS rating system. For banks providing fiduciary products and services, the UITRS must be updated during the supervisory cycle. For each significant line of business or activity, examiners should reach conclusions on the assessment standards for transaction risk, compliance risk, reputation risk, strategic risk, internal controls, and the applicable CAMELS and UITRS ratings during the 12-month supervisory cycle. In addition, the impact of asset management activities on the RAS should be updated or confirmed each quarter.

An examiner-in-charge (EIC) or a portfolio manager should maintain appropriate information about the asset management activities in their assigned banks to support the OCC's core knowledge, CAS, RAS, and supervisory strategy databases. The asset management examiner should work with the bank EIC or portfolio manager to develop and maintain an *asset management profile (AMP)* that includes the following information:

- A **business profile** that provides core knowledge about products and services, organizational structures, risk management systems, technology and information systems, strategic planning, and financial performance. A business profile may be necessary for each significant line of business.

- A **risk assessment profile** that uses the format and elements of the CAS and RAS and includes a summary of key asset management risks and the status of corrective action, if applicable. A risk assessment profile may be necessary for each significant line of business or support function.

- The **supervisory strategy** for asset management, including supervisory objectives, examination activities, and work plans. The strategy should be developed in accordance with the guidelines established for supervisory strategies in the "Large Bank Supervision" booklet of the *Comptroller's Handbook*.

The AMP should serve as the primary source of information for the core knowledge database, CAS, RAS, and other OCC electronic information systems. The profile format is flexible and should accommodate the many different organizational and supervisory structures that exist in national banks. For example, an organization that divides asset management activities into several distinct business units may require several AMPs. The number and format of AMPs is left to the discretion and judgment of each bank's EIC, but the content of an AMP should include the information described in the previous bullet points. Appendix B contains a sample format for an AMP.

Within 45 days of the end of each quarter, examiners should give the bank EIC an AMP update that should include, but not be limited to, the following:

- A summary of significant changes, if any, to the business and risk assessment profiles;

- A summary of examination activities completed or in process since the last update;

- A summary of meetings with bank managers, if applicable; and

- A strategic and financial performance overview of asset management activities.

Community Bank Supervision

Supervision of asset management activities in community banks is conducted in accordance with the guidelines established in the "Community Bank Supervision" and "Community Bank Fiduciary Activities Supervision" booklets of the *Comptroller's Handbook*. The "Community Bank Supervision" booklet includes discussions of core knowledge, CAS, RAS, supervisory strategy, and examination processes. The "Community Bank Fiduciary Activities Supervision" booklet provides examiners with specific guidance on how to conduct on-site fiduciary examinations. It includes the core assessment standards and expanded procedures applicable to fiduciary activities in community banks.

As of January 6, 2012, this guidance applies to federal savings associations in addition to national banks.*

Examination Procedures

Examiners use the OCC's core assessment standards (CAS) to reach minimum conclusions about a bank's risk profile and overall condition. The CAS for large banks are structured according to the RAS, the CAMELS rating system, and a section on internal controls. Asset management examiners provide information to the bank's EIC for input into the CAS during each supervisory cycle. The following expanded procedures provide examination guidance that is consistent with and supports the CAS for large banks and enables asset management examiners to complete supervisory activities consistently and effectively.

Supervising asset management activities involves assessing a large and complex variety of products, services, functions, processes, and information systems. The following expanded procedures provide examiner guidance for planning asset management supervisory activities, reaching overall conclusions on aggregate risks and risk management systems, and communicating conclusions and recommendations consistently with established OCC policies. To complete these procedures, the examiner must incorporate information from other asset management examination programs into overall conclusions about the quantity of risk and quality of risk management systems for asset management activities.

All key risk management and internal control functions must be periodically validated through transaction testing. The extent of testing and the procedures performed should be based on an assessment of risk. This assessment should include consideration of work performed by other regulatory agencies, internal and external auditors, compliance units, and the adequacy and effectiveness of internal controls and management information systems. Examiners should generally validate high-risk areas annually and low-risk areas every three years. Exceptions are permissible when adequately explained in the supervisory strategy.

General Procedures

The following procedures should be completed in conjunction with those used by the examiner responsible for planning and control of safety and soundness examination activities to avoid duplication and excessive burden on the bank.

Objective: Develop a preliminary assessment of the quantity of risk and the quality of risk management relating to asset management. This assessment should include appropriate risks and how asset management affects the direction and level of each risk. Use the assessment to finalize asset management examination activities and work plans in the supervisory cycle.

1. Determine the types and characteristics of the bank's asset management activities by obtaining and reviewing the following:

    ❑ OCC information databases.

    ❑ Previous reports of examination, analyses, and related board and management responses.

    ❑ The CAS and RAS.

    ❑ OCC correspondence files.

    ❑ Working papers from previous supervisory activities.

    ❑ Other applicable regulatory reports.

    ❑ Bank risk monitoring reports from committees, risk management groups, compliance, legal, and audit functions.

    ❑ Recent board and senior management reports relating to significant asset management activities.

2. Discuss the following with the bank's key risk managers:

    • Significant asset management risk issues and management plans.

- Significant changes in strategies, products, services, and distribution channels, including functionally regulated entities.

- Significant changes in organization, policies, controls, and information systems.

- External factors that are affecting asset management risk.

3. As appropriate, discuss asset management supervisory activities and previous risk assessments with the bank's EIC for perspective and strategy coordination. Consider the following:

  - Previous examination conclusions and recommendations.
  - Internal risk and control assessments.
  - Strategic and business plans.
  - New products, services, and distribution channels.
  - Changes in organization, policies, procedures, controls, and information systems.

The OCC's authority to examine subsidiaries and affiliates that are functionally regulated entities is limited. If the bank provides asset management products and services through an entity for which the OCC is not the primary functional regulator, discuss the appropriate supervisory approach that should be taken with the bank EIC and supervisory office prior to establishing the examination scope and work plan.

Objective: Establish the scope and work plans for asset management examination activities during the supervisory cycle.

1. Using the findings and analysis from the previous steps, and in consultation with the EIC and other appropriate regulatory agencies, determine the scope and specific work plans for the examination of asset management activities during the supervisory cycle. Prepare and submit a final planning memorandum for approval by the EIC that includes the following information:

  ❑ A preliminary risk assessment profile on asset management activities.

  ❑ A list of specific activities to be reviewed.

❑ The types (on-site and quarterly monitoring), schedules, and projected workdays of examination activities.

❑ The scope of examination procedures to be completed.

❑ The necessary examiner resources to complete the activities.

❑ The types of communication planned, such as meetings and final written products.

2.   Upon EIC approval of the planning memorandum,

- Select the asset management examination staff and make assignments consistent with the objectives, scope, and time frames of the planned examination activities;

- Discuss the examination plan with appropriate bank personnel and make suitable arrangements for on-site accommodations and additional information requests; and

- Contact each member of the examination team and provide necessary details concerning examination schedules and their individual assignment responsibilities.

These procedures should be performed in close consultation with the bank's EIC and with the EIC's authorization.

Note: If necessary, refer to the "Examination Planning and Control" and the "Large Bank Supervision" booklets of the *Comptroller's Handbook* for additional guidance on planning asset management examination activities.

Quantity of Risk

Transaction Risk

Conclusion: The quantity of transaction risk from asset management activities is (low, moderate, high).

Base your conclusion on the following core assessment factors:

	Low	Moderate	High
The volume, type, and complexity of transactions, products, and services offered through the bank.	❏	❏	❏
The condition, security, capacity, and recoverability of systems.	❏	❏	❏
The complexity of conversions, integrations, and system changes.	❏	❏	❏
The development of new markets, products, services, technology, and delivery systems in order to maintain competitive position and gain strategic advantage.	❏	❏	❏
The volume and severity of operational, administrative, and accounting control exceptions.	❏	❏	❏

Objective: To determine the quantity of transaction risk from the bank's delivery and administration of asset management products and services.

1. From the information obtained in the general procedures and other asset management examination activities, analyze the volume, types, and complexity of transactions, products, and services administered by the asset management lines of business and their impact on the quantity of transaction risk.

2. Obtain the results of the asset management information systems examination activities. Analyze and discuss the conclusions and recommendations with the assigned examiner(s).

3.   Review new and proposed products, services, and delivery systems and reach conclusions on how they affect information processing, accounting, and reporting systems.

4.   Obtain the results of the fiduciary operations and internal control examination programs, if applicable. Analyze and discuss the findings and recommendations with the assigned examiner(s).

5.   Reach a conclusion on the quantity of transaction risk from asset management activities based on the findings of these and other applicable asset management examination activities. Determine the impact on the assessment factors and assign a rating of low, moderate, or high to each applicable factor.

Compliance Risk

Conclusion: The quantity of compliance risk from asset management activities is (low, moderate, high).

Base your conclusion on the following core assessment factors:

	Low	Moderate	High
Business Activity	❏	❏	❏

The nature and extent of business activities include new products and services.

	Low	Moderate	High
Noncompliance	❏	❏	❏

The volume and significance of noncompliance and nonconformance with policies and procedures, laws, regulations, prescribed practices, and ethical standards.

	Low	Moderate	High
Litigation	❏	❏	❏

The amount and significance of litigation and customer complaints.

Objective: To determine the quantity of compliance risk from the bank's delivery and administration of asset management products and services.

1. Obtain and analyze the types and volume of asset management products and services, including proposed new products and services. Consider information from the following sources:

    ☐ Internal management information reports.
    ☐ FFIEC trust reports
    ☐ SEC report filings.
    ☐ Call reports.

2. Obtain and analyze the types and level of policy exceptions, internal control deficiencies, and law violations that have been identified and reported internally. Review the following information sources:

    ☐ Risk management division reports.
    ☐ Compliance reports.
    ☐ Self-assessment program reports.
    ☐ Internal and external audit reports.
    ☐ Regulatory reports.
    ☐ Other OCC examination programs.

3. Obtain and analyze the types and volume of litigation and consumer complaints related to asset management activities.

4. Discuss significant litigation and complaints with management and determine the risk to capital and the appropriateness of corrective action and follow-up processes. Refer to the "Litigation and Other Legal Matters" booklet of the *Comptroller's Handbook* for additional procedures.

5. Reach a conclusion on the quantity of compliance risk from asset management activities based on the findings of these and other asset management examination activities. Determine the impact on each assessment factor and assign a rating of low, moderate, or high to each factor.

Strategic Risk

Conclusion: Aggregate strategic risk from asset management activities is (low, moderate, high).

Base your conclusion on the following core assessment factors:

	Low	Moderate	High
Strategic Factors	☐	☐	☐

- The magnitude of change in established corporate mission, goals, culture, values, or risk tolerance.

- The financial objectives as they relate to the short-term and long-term goals of the bank.

- The market situation, including product, customer demographics, and geographic position.

- Diversification by product, geography, and customer demographics.

- Past performance in offering new products and services.

- Merger and acquisition plans and opportunities.

- Potential or planned entrance into new businesses or product lines.

	Low	Moderate	High
External Factors	☐	☐	☐

- The impact of economic, industry, and market conditions; legislative and regulatory change; technological advances; and competition.

	Low	Moderate	High
Management, Processes, and Systems	☐	☐	☐

- The expertise of senior management and the effectiveness of the board of directors.

- The priority of personnel, technology, and capital resources allocation and their compatibility with strategic initiatives.

- Past performance in offering new products or services and evaluating potential and consummated acquisitions.

- The effectiveness of management methods of communicating, implementing, and modifying strategic plans, and consistency with stated risk tolerance.

- The accuracy, quality, and integrity of management information systems.

- The adequacy and independence of controls to monitor business decisions.

- The responsiveness to deficiencies in internal controls.

- The quality and integrity of reports to the board of directors necessary to oversee strategic decisions.

Objective: To determine the aggregate level of strategic risk from the bank's delivery and administration of asset management products and services.

1. Obtain and analyze the bank's strategic plan relating to asset management activities. Consider each of the strategic factors listed above and reach a conclusion of low, moderate, or high.

2. Discuss with management the impact of the external factors listed above on the bank's strategic plan and reach conclusions of low, moderate, or high.

3. Obtain and analyze information from the risk management procedural section and other applicable examination activities relating to the management, processes, and systems factors. Discuss these factors with management and other examiners and reach a conclusion on the aggregate level of strategic risk from asset management activities.

Reputation Risk

Conclusion: Aggregate reputation risk from asset management activities is (low, moderate, high).

Base your conclusion on the following core assessment factors:

	Low	Moderate	High
Strategic Factors	❏	❏	❏

- The volume of assets and number of accounts under management or administration.

- Merger and acquisition plans and opportunities.

- Potential or planned entrance into new businesses or product lines, particularly those that test legal boundaries.

	Low	Moderate	High
External Factors	❏	❏	❏

- The market or public perception of the corporate mission, culture, and risk tolerance of the bank.

- The market or public perception of the bank's financial stability.

- The market or public perception of the quality of products and services offered by the bank.

- The impact of economic, industry, and market conditions; legislative and regulatory change; technological advances; and competition.

	Low	Moderate	High
Management, Processes, and Systems	❏	❏	❏

- Past performance in offering new products or services and in conducting due diligence prior to start-up.

- The nature and amount of litigation and the nature and number of customer complaints.

- The expertise of senior management and the effectiveness of the board of directors in maintaining an ethical, self-policing culture.

- Management's willingness and ability to adjust strategies based on regulatory changes, market disruptions, market or public perception, and legal losses.

- The quality and integrity of management information systems and the development of expanded or newly integrated systems.

- The adequacy and independence of controls used to monitor business decisions.

- The responsiveness to deficiencies in internal controls.

- The ability to minimize exposure from litigation and customer complaints.

- The ability to communicate effectively with the market, public, and media.

- Management responsiveness to internal and regulatory review findings.

Objective: To determine aggregate reputation risk from the bank's delivery and administration of asset management products and services.

1. Discuss with management the impact of the strategic factors listed above on the bank's reputation and reach a conclusion of low, moderate, or high.

2. Discuss with management the impact of the external factors listed above on the bank's reputation and reach a conclusion of low, moderate, or high.

3. Obtain and analyze information from the risk management procedural section and other applicable examination activities relating to the management, processes, and systems factors. Discuss these factors with management and other examiners and reach a conclusion on the aggregate level of reputation risk from asset management activities.

Quality of Risk Management

Conclusion: The quality of risk management relating to asset management activities is (strong, satisfactory, weak).

Policies

Conclusion: The board has (strong, satisfactory, weak) asset management policies.

Consider the following factors:

- The consistency of policies with the strategic direction of the bank.

- The structure of the bank's operations and whether responsibility and accountability are assigned at every level.

- The reasonableness of definitions that determine policy exceptions.

- The periodic review and approval of policies by the board or an appropriate committee.

- The reasonableness of guidelines that establish risk limits or positions.

- The structure of the compliance operation and whether responsibility and accountability are assigned at every level.

Objective: To determine whether the board, or a designated committee, has adopted asset management policies that maintain compliance with applicable law, establish and promote sound risk management practices, and are consistent with risk tolerance standards.

1. Identify and obtain asset management policies, including those related to information systems, and, if applicable, distribute the policies to examiners responsible for examining specific asset management activities.

2. Review the policies and determine whether they

- Are reviewed and formally approved by the board or its designated committee;

- Address applicable law;

- Outline the bank's unique asset management goals and objectives, ethical culture, risk tolerance standards, and risk management strategies;

- Address all significant asset management activities and, when appropriate, include policies for

  - Securities trading, including brokerage placement practices;
  - Use of material inside information with securities transactions;
  - Conflicts of interest and self-dealing;
  - Selection and retention of legal counsel;
  - Investment of fiduciary funds; and
  - Retail nondeposit investment sales.

- Include appropriate guidelines for

  - Communicating policies and subsequent policy changes;
  - Monitoring policy compliance and reporting exceptions; and
  - Policy review and approval by the board, or its designated committee, at least annually.

3. Obtain and review the bank's policies relating to information processing, security, and contingency planning. Determine whether asset management activities are adequately addressed in such policies. Consider information in related OCC issuances, including:

- OCC Bulletin 97-23, "FFIEC Interagency Statement on Corporate Business Resumption and Contingency Planning";

- OCC Bulletin 98-3, "Technology Risk Management";

- OCC Bulletin 98-38, "Technology Risk Management: PC Banking";

- OCC Bulletin 99-9, "Infrastructure Threats from Cyber-Terrorists";

- OCC Banking Circular 226, "End-User Computing"; and

- OCC Banking Circular 229, "Information Security."

4. Evaluate the policy review process and determine whether changes in risk tolerance, strategic direction, products and services, or the external environment are adequately and effectively considered by the process.

5. Through discussion with management and other examiners, identify asset management policies that need development or revision. Consider the following:

- Recently developed and distributed products and services;
- Discontinued products, services, organizational structures, and information systems; and
- Recent updates or revisions to existing policies and procedures.

6. Draw a final conclusion on the bank's asset management policy formulation and adoption system by reviewing the findings of these and other applicable examination activities and through discussions with management.

Processes

Conclusion: The bank has (strong, satisfactory, weak) processes for managing asset management risks and achieving its financial goals and objectives.

Consider the following factors:

- The adequacy of processes communicating policies and expectations to appropriate personnel;

- The approval and monitoring of compliance with policies;

- The appropriateness of the approval process;

- Management responsiveness to regulatory, industry, and technological changes;

- The incorporation of project management into daily operations (e.g., systems development, capacity, change control, due diligence, and outsourcing);

- The adequacy of processes defining the systems architecture for transaction processing and for delivering products and services;

- The adequacy of systems to monitor capacity and performance;

- The effectiveness of processes developed to ensure the integrity and security of systems and the independence of operating staff;

- The adequacy of system documentation history;

- The adequacy of processes to ensure the reliability and retention of information, including business continuity planning (i.e., data creation, processing, storage, and delivery);

- The adequacy of controls over new product development;

- The adequacy of data systems and reports;

- The adequacy of management supervision and board oversight;

- The adequacy of internal controls, including segregation of duties and dual controls;

- The provision of timely and useful management information systems reports;

- The effectiveness of processes controlling the accuracy, completeness, and integrity of data;

- The adequacy of processes assimilating legislative and regulatory changes into all aspects of the company;

- The commitment to ensuring that appropriate resources are allocated to training and compliance;

- The extent to which violations or noncompliance are identified internally and corrected; and

- The adequacy of integrating compliance considerations into all phases of corporate planning.

Objective: To determine the quality of asset management strategic planning processes that have been adopted by the board and management.

1. Evaluate the bank's asset management strategic planning process. Consider the following:

- Is the asset management planning process part of the bank's overall strategic and financial planning processes? If so, document the process through the following procedures and provide this information to other examiners, as applicable.

- Does the process require the formulation and adoption of a long-term strategic plan supported by short-term business plans? Consider the following:

  - Annual financial business plans/budgets.
  - Capital plan.
  - Asset/liability plan.
  - Marketing plan.
  - Staffing and training plan.
  - Information technology systems plan.
  - Fixed asset planning.

- Does the process require periodic assessment, updating, and re-affirmations by the board and management of the asset management strategic and business plans?

- Does the process consider all significant elements of risk that affect asset management activities, such as internal risk tolerance standards, the corporate ethical culture, available financial resources, management expertise, technology capabilities, operating systems, competition, economic and market conditions, and legal and regulatory issues?

- Does the planning process consider asset management risks when assessing institutional capital needs or allocations? Consider the following:

  - Pending litigation.
  - Establishment of reserves for losses.
  - Insurance coverage reviews.
  - Risk management processes.

- Does the process include an effective means of communicating strategies, financial performance goals, and risk tolerance philosophy? Consider the following:

  - Communication techniques used.
  - Timeliness and adequacy of communications.
  - Formality of communications.
  - Audience awareness of the communications (directors, senior managers, middle managers, employees).

- Are policies and procedures consistent with the strategic plan?

2. Evaluate how management implements the strategic plan and monitors and reports performance to the board, or its designated committee. Consider the following:

- Are the development, implementation, and monitoring of short-term business plans consistent with board-established planning processes?

- Are management processes adequate and effective?

- Does management submit periodic reports to the board, or its designated committee, that provide accurate, reliable, understandable and relevant information about the following:

  - Success in meeting strategic goals and objectives.

  - Quantity and direction of asset management risks.

  - Adequacy of risk management systems.

  - Financial performance analyses, including the adequacy of capital allocated to the business lines.

  - Summaries of changes to risk and business strategies, corrective actions, and proposed recommendations to address excessive risk levels or remedy control weaknesses.

Objective: To determine the quality of asset management risk assessment processes used by the board and management.

1.   Evaluate the processes used by the board and management to identify, estimate, and report risks from asset management activities. Consider the following:

- Processes for selecting, educating, and evaluating directors and senior managers responsible for asset management oversight through committee membership and participation.

- Quality and effectiveness of risk assessment systems and models to determine the level of risk for each product or function.

- Processes to incorporate asset management risks into the assessment of institutional capital requirements.

- Processes for monitoring compliance with policies, procedures, and internal controls. Consider the following:

  - Board and committee minutes relating to asset management.
  - Quality of management information systems.
  - Communication techniques and channels.
  - Risk management, audit, and compliance reporting processes.
  - Policy and internal control exception reporting processes.
  - Regulatory examination report reviews.

- Account acceptance and termination processes.

- Processes for pricing products and services.

- Insurance selection and review processes.

- Litigation and consumer complaints review processes.

- Information systems and management reports.

- Financial performance and trends analyses.

- Regulatory reporting and awareness processes.

- Technology management processes.

Objective: To determine whether the board and management have adopted and implemented an organizational structure that is consistent with strategic goals and the risk profile of the institution's asset management activities.

1. Determine how asset management activities are organized and if clear lines of authority and responsibility for monitoring adherence to policies, procedures, and processes are established. Consider the following:

   - Bank bylaws and resolutions.
   - Strategic plan and business strategies.
   - Board and management committees.
   - Management structures.
   - Other organizational structures.

2. If the board has delegated fiduciary supervision to a committee, review such committee's composition, charter, meeting frequency, attendance, information reports, and board reporting processes for consistency with board guidance and regulatory requirements.

Objective: To determine the quality of operating procedures that management has adopted to implement asset management business strategies and policies and ensure compliance with applicable law.

1. Review the findings and recommendations of other asset management examination programs and reach overall conclusions on the quality of asset management operating procedures.

2. Evaluate the processes used by management to ensure compliance with policies, procedures, internal controls, and applicable law, and initiate and enforce corrective action. Consider the following:

   - The quality and timeliness of management information reports.
   - Responsiveness to reports from risk management, audit, compliance, and regulatory organizations.
   - Control self-assessment programs.
   - Personnel practices and training programs.

- Communication processes.
- Policy and internal control exception tracking systems.

Objective: To determine the quality of internal controls.

1. Draw conclusions on internal controls for asset management activities after reviewing the findings of other examination programs, particularly the fiduciary operations and internal controls examination program. Submit the final assessment of asset management internal controls to the examiner responsible for evaluating internal controls of the entire bank. Use the following format:

	Strong	Satisfactory	Weak
Control environment	❐	❐	❐
Risk assessment	❐	❐	❐
Control activities	❐	❐	❐
Accounting, information, and communication	❐	❐	❐
Self-assessment and monitoring	❐	❐	❐

The overall system of internal controls for asset management activities is:

Strong	Satisfactory	Weak
❐	❐	❐

2. If necessary, and if approved by the bank EIC and internal control examiner, complete appropriate examination procedures in the "Internal Control" booklet of the *Comptroller's Handbook.*

Objective: To evaluate the quality of product development, marketing, and risk assessment processes.

1. Determine how management assesses the types and level of risk in asset management products and services.

2. Determine and evaluate how management plans for new products and services. Consider the following:

- Types of market research conducted, such as product feasibility studies.
- Cost, pricing, and profitability analyses.
- Risk assessment processes.
- Legal counsel and review.
- Role of risk management and audit functions.
- Information systems and technology impact.
- Human resource impact.

Objective: To determine the quality of asset management information security systems and controls.

1. Review asset management information systems security control processes. Refer to OCC Banking Circular 229, "Information Security," for guidance on appropriate control processes.

2. Evaluate board and management processes for monitoring information security policies, procedures, and control systems.

Objective: To determine the quality of third-party vendor selection and monitoring processes.

1. Review policies and processes for the selection and monitoring of third-party vendors. Discuss the process with management and document significant risk management weaknesses. Consider the following:

- Vendor due diligence review process.
- Contract negotiation and approval process.
- Risk assessment process.
- Risk management and audit division participation.
- Vendor monitoring processes, such as the frequency and quality of information reviewed.

  - For data processing services, determine whether the board, or a designated committee, performs an annual review of financial information on the vendor. See OCC Banking Circular 187, "Financial Information on Data Processing Servicers," for guidance.

- Vendor problem resolution process.

Refer to OCC Advisory Letter 2000-9, "Third-Party Risk," for guidance.

Refer to the "Retail Nondeposit Investment Sales" section of the *Comptroller's Handbook for National Bank Examiners* for examination guidance on arrangements with third-party vendors in this line of business.

Objective: To determine the quality of legal counsel selection and evaluation processes and processes established for managing litigation and consumer complaints.

1. Analyze the selection and evaluation process for legal counsel.

2. Discuss with management its level of satisfaction with the performance of legal counsel.

3. Determine whether management uses legal counsel appropriately and effectively by reviewing the following:

   - The volume and status of current and pending litigation, claims, or assessments;
   - Governing instruments involving unclear, ambiguous, or complicated points of law; and
   - Transactions involving possible conflicts of interest.

4. Review the consumer complaint resolution process for adequacy and effectiveness.

5. Review significant consumer complaints and determine whether management is responding appropriately and consistently with internal processes.

6. Reach final conclusions and forward to the examiner responsible for assessing pending litigation and other legal matters.

Personnel

Conclusion: The bank has (strong, satisfactory, weak) management, supporting staff, and personnel policies and programs.

Consider the following factors:

- The appropriateness of performance management and compensation programs.

- The degree of turnover of critical staff.

- The adequacy of training.

- The extent of managerial expertise.

- The understanding and adherence to the strategic direction and risk tolerance as defined by senior management and the board.

Objective: To determine the quality and sufficiency of the bank's management and supporting personnel.

1. Review the experience, education, and other training of managers and key supporting personnel. The review should include personnel from the business line, risk management, fiduciary committees, compliance, audit, information systems, and any other areas that play a significant role in risk management. Determine whether personnel are

   - Adequate based on the bank's asset management risk characteristics.

   - Compatible and consistent with asset management and corporate strategic initiatives.

   - Knowledgeable of the bank's asset management policies, strategic plans, and risk tolerance standards.

   - Aware of the bank's code of ethics, if applicable, and demonstrate a strong commitment to high ethical standards.

2. Review recent staffing analyses prepared by management for applicable asset management business lines and evaluate the adequacy of staffing levels by considering

- Current strategic initiatives and financial goals.
- Current business volume, complexity, and risk profile.
- The impact of company-initiated cost-cutting programs.

3. Compare job descriptions and other responsibilities of managers and key supporting personnel with their experience, education, and other training.

    - Are personnel qualified and adequately trained for positions and responsibilities?

    - Are personnel performing tasks outside their job descriptions that are affecting their overall performance?

Objective: To determine the quality of the bank's personnel policies, practices, and programs.

1. Determine whether lines of authority and individual duties and responsibilities are clearly defined and communicated.

2. Evaluate the bank's asset management recruitment and employee retention program. Consider the following:

    - Recent success in hiring and retaining high-quality personnel.
    - Level and trends of staff turnover, particularly in key positions.
    - The quality and reasonableness of management succession plans.

3. Analyze asset management compensation and performance evaluation programs by considering the following:

    - Is the compensation and performance evaluation program appropriate for the types of products and services offered?

    - Is the program formalized and periodically reviewed by the board and senior management?

    - Is the program competitive with industry standards and consistent with the bank's risk tolerance and ethical standards?

- Are responsibilities and accountability standards clearly established for the performance evaluation program?

- Is the program applied consistently and functioning as intended?

- Does the program reward behavior and performance that is consistent with the bank's ethical culture, risk tolerance standards, and strategic initiatives?

- Does the program include an adequate mechanism for the board to evaluate management performance?

4. Review the asset management training program by considering the following:

- The types and frequency of training and whether the program is adequate and effective.

- How much of the asset management budget is allocated to training and whether the financial resources applied to asset management training are adequate.

- If employee training needs and accomplishments are a component of the performance evaluation program.

Control Systems

Conclusion: The bank has (strong, satisfactory, weak) asset management control and monitoring systems.

Consider the following factors:

- The effectiveness and independence of the risk review, quality assurance, and audit functions.

- The accuracy, completeness, and integrity of management information systems and reports.

- The existence of exception monitoring systems that identify and measure incremental risk by how much (in frequency and amount) the exceptions deviate from policy and established limits.

- The responsiveness to identified internal deficiencies in policies, processes, personnel, and internal controls.

- The independent testing of processes to ensure ongoing reliability and integrity.

Objective: To determine the quality of asset management control and monitoring systems.

1.   Determine and evaluate the types of control systems used by the board and management. Consider the following:

   - Committee structure and operation.
   - Risk management functions.
   - Compliance program.
   - Audit program.
   - Management information systems.
   - Quantitative risk measurement systems.
   - Control self-assessment processes.

2.   Determine the extent to which the board and senior management are involved in risk control and monitoring processes. Evaluate the

   - Types and frequency of board and senior management reviews used to determine adherence to policies and procedures.

   - Adequacy, timeliness, and distribution of management information reports.

   - Responsiveness to risk control deficiencies and effectiveness of correction action and follow-up activities.

   - Asset management committee structure: organization, membership, charters, information reports, meeting schedule, attendance, and follow-up on critical risk control issues.

   - Quality and effectiveness of account acceptance and review processes.

3.   Evaluate the adequacy and effectiveness of risk assessment models and how management uses them to control and monitor risk.

4.   If the bank has a separate risk management function for asset management activities, review its purpose, structure, reporting process, and effectiveness. Consider the following:

   • Size, complexity, strategic plans, and trends in asset management activities.

   • Objectivity or relationship to risk-taking activities.

   • Quality and quantity of personnel.

   • Quality of risk assessment, transaction testing, monitoring systems, and reporting processes.

5.   Evaluate the asset management compliance program. Consider the following:

   • Extent of board and senior management commitment and support.

   • Line management responsibility and accountability.

   • Formalization, transaction testing, reporting structures, and follow-up processes.

   • Qualifications and performance of compliance officer and supporting personnel.

   • Communication systems.

   • Training programs.

6.   If the bank has implemented a control self-assessment program, obtain information on the asset management component of the program. Evaluate the program and the results of recent control self-assessments of asset management activities.

7.   Review the bank's asset management audit program and reach a conclusion on the program's adequacy and effectiveness. In the course of the review,

- Select and complete appropriate examination procedures from the "Internal and External Audits" booklet of the *Comptroller's Handbook*, coordinating your work with the examiner responsible for the bank's audit program.

- Obtain appropriate internal and external audit and follow-up reports, including audits of functionally regulated subsidiaries and affiliates, and disseminate the reports to the appropriate examiners for review and follow-up.

- Determine the adequacy and effectiveness of audit programs relating to asset management by reviewing:

  - The qualifications and competency of the audit staff.
  - The timing, scope, and results of audit activity.
  - The quality of audit reports and follow-up processes.

- Draw conclusions about the adequacy and effectiveness of audit programs relating to asset management and forward the findings and recommendations, if applicable, to the examiner(s) responsible for evaluating the bank's audit program.

Conclusions

Objective: To consolidate the conclusions and recommendations from the various asset management examination activities into final conclusions on the quantity of risk and quality of risk management.

1.   Obtain conclusion memoranda and other risk assessment products from completed asset management examination activities.

2.   Discuss the individual examination findings with the responsible examiner(s) and ensure that conclusions and recommendations are accurate, supported, and appropriately communicated.

3.   Determine and document the appropriate fiduciary composite and management ratings using the factors listed in the UITRS and the findings from the other fiduciary examination activities.

4.   Finalize asset management risk and risk management conclusions for input into the following:

- Core knowledge database
- Core assessment standards (CAS)
- Risk assessment system (RAS)
- Uniform Interagency Trust Rating System (UITRS)
- CAMELS
- Report of examination
- Asset management profile (AMP)

Objective: To communicate examination findings and initiate corrective action, if applicable.

1.   Provide the EIC the following information, when applicable:

- Conclusions on the impact of asset management activities on the applicable CAS, including the CAMELS and internal controls sections.

- Conclusions on the impact of asset management activities on the applicable RAS factors.

- UITRS ratings recommendations.

- Draft report of examination comments.

- Matters requiring attention (MRA).

- Violations of law and regulation.

- Other recommendations provided to bank management.

2. Discuss examination findings and revised AMP with the EIC and adjust findings and recommendations as needed. If the fiduciary composite or management rating is 3 or worse, or the level of any risk factor is moderate and increasing or high due to the impact of asset management activities, contact the supervisory office before conducting the exit meeting with management.

3. Hold an exit meeting with appropriate asset management committees and/or risk managers to communicate examination conclusions and obtain commitments for corrective action, if applicable. Allow management time before the meeting to review draft examination conclusions and report comments. Meetings with the board should be scheduled only with the explicit approval of the EIC and the supervisory office.

4. Prepare final comments for inclusion in the report of examination as requested by the EIC. Perform a final check to determine whether comments

- Meet OCC report of examination guidelines.
- Support assigned UITRS ratings.
- Contain accurate citations of violations.

5. If there are MRA comments, enter them into the OCC's electronic information system. Ensure that the comments are consistent with MRA content requirements.

6. Enter the fiduciary examination report comments into the appropriate OCC electronic file. Supplement the analysis comment, when appropriate, to include:

- The objectives and scope of fiduciary supervisory activities.

- Reasons for changes in the supervisory strategy, if applicable.

- Overall conclusions, recommendations for corrective action, and management commitments and time frames.

- Comments on recommended administrative actions, enforcement actions, and/or civil money penalty referrals.

7. Update applicable sections of electronic supervisory information systems, including:

    - UITRS ratings.
    - RAS (if requested by the bank EIC).
    - Violations of law or regulation.
    - Core knowledge database.

8. Prepare a recommended asset management supervisory strategy for the subsequent supervisory cycle and provide to the EIC for review and approval.

9. Prepare a memorandum or update work programs with any information that will facilitate future examinations.

10. Organize and reference work papers in accordance with OCC guidelines.

11. Complete and distribute assignment evaluations for assisting examiners.

Appendix A: Operating a Risk Management Unit

This appendix discusses how to organize and operate a risk management unit to support asset management lines of business. The information presented is a summary from a survey completed by the OCC of fiduciary risk management functions in large banks.

The risk management function should be formalized.

While no one risk management structure is appropriate for all banks, effective programs are usually formalized and well-documented. Risk management functions for asset management services are generally organized in one of three forms:

1. *A risk management unit independent of the business line.*

Although the day-to-day responsibility for managing risk lies with business line managers, many banks have established risk management divisions that operate independently from the line function. An independent risk management division can be a valuable tool for assessing and reporting on risk levels and control systems within the framework of a comprehensive, corporate-wide risk management function.

2. *A risk management unit integrated into the business line.*

In this framework, risk managers report administratively to business line executives and work closely with the business units to manage risk. This structure allows risk managers to be proactive and closer to current risk issues and concerns. It also expedites problem correction.

3. *A risk management unit that, while part of the business line, has "dotted-line" reporting to an independent risk management group.*

Some risk managers may report to the asset management business executive and to the corporate risk management supervisor. This hybrid approach provides aspects of independence, closer interaction with line management, and daily evaluation of risk.

Basic duties and responsibilities of the risk management function should be formally established.

A risk manager or risk management unit generally does the following:

- Educates bank employees about risk management principles.
- Assists line management with risk assessments.
- Coordinates risk management across functional lines.
- Prioritizes risk management issues.
- Assists or advises on the development of policies, procedures, limits, and other control systems.
- Identifies, estimates, and reports risk exposures.
- Monitors the status of corrective action on deficiencies cited by auditors, compliance personnel, line management, and regulators.

Asset management business line managers should be responsible and accountable for risk management.

The success of risk management depends on how well risk management practices are integrated into the daily operations of asset management services. By making line management accountable for daily risk management processes, the program becomes a continuous process occurring at the transaction and portfolio levels. Issues or concerns can be identified within the business line. This results in line management having a better understanding of business unit risks and the importance of risk management. A well-designed risk management function enables the board to hold management accountable for complying with established risk limits.

Risk management should be a continuous process.

Risk management should be continuously implemented and evaluated. To remain effective and useful, risk management processes must be continuously updated to reflect changes in a bank's risk strategies and operations.

Regardless of the organizational framework established for a risk management function, directors and senior management should be confident that risk management personnel are performing their duties impartially and are not being unduly influenced by business line managers.

Appendix B: Asset Management Profile — Sample Format

Bank Name:
Examiner-in-charge:
Preparer:

Section 1. Business Profile

Products, Services, and/or Function

Organizational Structure

Risk Management Systems

- Supervision
- Policies
- Processes
- Personnel
- Control and monitoring systems

  - ☐ Committees
  - ☐ Risk management function
  - ☐ Compliance program
  - ☐ Self-assessment program
  - ☐ Management information reporting systems
  - ☐ Audit program

Technology and Information Systems

Financial Performance

Section 2.   Risk Assessment Profile

I.   Risk Assessment System

Risk	Quantity	Quality	Aggregate	Direction
Transaction				
Compliance				
Strategic				
Reputation				

Provide comments addressing the quantity of risk, quality of risk management, aggregate risk, and direction of risk for each category affected by asset management activities. Include a list of key issues and the status of correction action, if applicable.

Transaction Risk

Compliance Risk

Strategic Risk

Reputation Risk

Include other risks, if appropriate.

II.   Core Assessment Standards

Quantity of Transaction Risk	Low	Moderate	High
The volume, type, and complexity of transactions, products and services offered through the bank.	❏	❏	❏
The condition, security, capacity, and recoverability of systems.	❏	❏	❏

	Low	Moderate	High
The complexity of conversions, integrations, and system changes.	❏	❏	❏
The development of new markets, products, services, technology, and delivery systems in order to maintain competitive position and gain strategic advantage	❏	❏	❏
The volume and severity of operational, administrative, and accounting control exceptions.	❏	❏	❏

Quantity of Compliance Risk	Low	Moderate	High
Business activity	❏	❏	❏
Noncompliance	❏	❏	❏
Litigation	❏	❏	❏

Quantity of Strategic Risk	Low	Moderate	High
Strategic factors	❏	❏	❏
External factors	❏	❏	❏
Management, processes, and systems	❏	❏	❏

Quantity of Reputation Risk	Low	Moderate	High
Strategic factors	❏	❏	❏
External factors	❏	❏	❏
Management, processes, and systems	❏	❏	❏

Quality of Risk Management	Strong	Satisfactory	Weak
Policies	❏	❏	❏
Processes	❏	❏	❏
Personnel	❏	❏	❏
Control systems	❏	❏	❏

Internal Controls	Strong	Satisfactory	Weak

Control environment	☐	☐	☐
Risk Assessment	☐	☐	☐
Control activities	☐	☐	☐
Accounting, information, and communication	☐	☐	☐
Self-assessment and monitoring	☐	☐	☐
The overall system of internal controls is:	☐	☐	☐

III. CAMELS

Provide comments that address the impact of asset management risks and risk management systems on the interagency rating system.

Composite

- Capital
- Asset Quality
- Management
- Earnings
- Liquidity
- Sensitivity to Market Risk

IV. Uniform Interagency Trust Rating System

	1	2	3	4	5
Management	☐	☐	☐	☐	☐
Operations, internal controls, and auditing	☐	☐	☐	☐	☐
Earnings	☐	☐	☐	☐	☐
Compliance	☐	☐	☐	☐	☐
Asset management	☐	☐	☐	☐	☐
Composite Rating	☐	☐	☐	☐	☐

Section 3.   SUPERVISORY STRATEGY

I.   **Supervisory Cycle:**

II.   **Objectives:**

III.   **Activities:**

IV.   **Work Plans:**

As of January 6, 2012, this guidance applies to federal savings associations in addition to national banks.*

References

Laws

12 USC 92a, Trust Powers of National Banks
The Gramm-Leach-Bliley Act of 1999
Securities Act of 1933
Securities Exchange Act of 1934
Investment Company Act of 1940
Investment Advisors Act of 1940
Employee Retirement Income Security Act of 1974 (ERISA)
The Bank Secrecy Act
Internal Revenue Code

Regulations

12 CFR 5.26, Corporate Activities, Fiduciary Powers
12 CFR 9, Fiduciary Activities of National Banks
12 CFR 12, Record Keeping and Confirmation Requirements for Securities Transactions
12 CFR 21, Minimum Security Devices and Procedures, Reports of Suspicious Activities, and Bank Secrecy Act Compliance Program
12 CFR 28, International Banking Activities
12 CFR 30, Safety and Soundness Standards
12 CFR 40, Privacy of Consumer Financial Information
31 CFR 103, Financial Record Keeping and Reporting of Currency and Foreign Transactions

Treatises

Restatement of the Law, Trusts, 2nd and 3rd, The American Law Institute
Scott and Fratcher, The Law of Trusts (4th edition, 1988)

Comptroller's Handbook Booklets

"Bank Supervision Process"
"Large Bank Supervision"
"Community Bank Supervision"
"Community Bank Fiduciary Activities Supervision"
"Examination Planning and Control"
"Sampling Methodologies"
"Internal Control"
"Internal and External Audits"
"Conflicts of Interest"
"Litigation and Other Legal Matters"

As of January 6, 2012, this guidance applies to federal savings associations in addition to national banks.*

"Management Information Systems"
"Consumer Compliance Examination"
"Federal Branches and Agencies Supervision"

OCC Issuances

Comptroller's Corporate Manual
Advisory Letter 2000-9, "Third-Party Risk"
Advisory Letter 2000-6, "Audit and Internal Controls"
Advisory Letter 2000-3, "Bank Secrecy Act Compliance Programs — Suspicious Activity Reporting Requirements"
OCC Bulletin 2000-26, "Supervision of National Trust Banks"
OCC Bulletin 2000-25, "Privacy Laws and Regulations"
OCC Bulletin 2000-16, "Risk Modeling-Model Validation"
OCC Bulletin 2000-11, "Financial Subsidiaries and Operating Subsidiaries- Final Rule"
OCC Bulletin 98-46, "Uniform Interagency Trust Rating System"
OCC Bulletin 98-01, "Interagency Policy Statement-Internal Audit/Outsourcing"
OCC Bulletin 97-22, "Fiduciary Activities of National Banks. Q & A's 12 CFR 9"
OCC Bulletin 95-52, "Retail Sales of Nondeposit Investment Products — Clarification of Interagency Guidelines"
OCC Bulletin 94-13, "Nondeposit Investment Sales Examination Procedures"
Interpretive Letter 872, "Authority of a National Bank To Engage in Fiduciary Activities in Other States"
Interpretive Letter 866, "Authority of a National Bank To Market Fiduciary Services to, and Act as Fiduciary for, Customers in Various States"
Interpretive Letter 695, "Authority of a National Bank To Conduct Fiduciary Activities on a Nationwide Basis through Trust Offices in Various States"

www.ingramcontent.com/pod-product-compliance
Lightning Source LLC
Chambersburg PA
CBHW080320290526
45790CB00005B/2123